Conversation Gambits

Eric Keller and Sylvia T Warner

Real English Conversation Practices

Conversation Circles

P. 32-33 #23 ⎱ 1 week
34 #24 ⎰

Think of personal examples.
Directions to place in the city.
store in the mall

Photocopy (this)

CONVERSATION GAMBITS
✓70 - 73 5 copies
✓74 - 75 5 copies
76 - 77 5 copies

Language Teaching Publications

Contents

3. Responding Gambits

To the Student

How natural is your conversation in English?

The main way we make our conversation sound natural is by using 'gambits'. A gambit is a word or phrase which helps us to express what we are trying to say. For example, we use gambits to introduce a topic of conversation; to link what we have to say to what someone has just said; to agree or disagree; to respond to what we have heard. In one sense, a gambit has very little meaning — it does not express an opinion; it may only introduce the opinion. On the other hand, if we never use gambits in our conversation, other people will think we are very direct, abrupt, and even rude — they will get a wrong picture of us as people So gambits are full of meaning. They show our attitude to the person we are speaking to and to what (s)he is saying.

We could go into a shop and ask, How much is this? But it is more natural and pleasant if we ask, *Could you tell me how much this is please*? If you have just heard that your teacher is going to get married, you could walk into the class and announce the fact, but you will have more effect if you start, *Are you sitting down? You won't believe this but our teacher is getting married.*

If you want to express a deeply-held belief, people will understand you better if you start, I *personally feel that* . . . — and if you think your view is surprising, people will react better if you introduce it with, *Not everyone will agree with me, but I think (we should bring back hanging).* Gambits will make your English sound more natural, more confident, and will make you easier to talk to. Above all, you will not be misunderstood.

The activities

In each of the activities you are asked to work in pairs or small groups to have conversations. In each activity there is a list of gambits at the side. Before you start your conversation, make sure you can say them. Try to use them in your conversations. If you find them difficult, have the conversation again and try to use them. It will help you if, after your conversation, you try to write it down and include the gambits. Then read aloud what you have written. Do not try to memorise the gambits. You will remember them better if you try to involve yourself in the activities in an active way. Ask your teacher if you sound natural when you use them. Above all, try to use them whenever you have an English conversation outside the classroom.

Remember, for these activities the gambits are as important as the content of your conversation!

The last activity (63. **Mini-conversations**) includes a list of subjects for discussion which you can use for ideas in many of the activities.

1. Opening Gambits

We use opening gambits to help us introduce ideas into the conversation. The beginning of a conversation is usually the most difficult part for most people. If we start in a natural and friendly way, we will most likely have a positive meeting. If we start 'on the wrong foot', we may be misunderstood.

We use opening gambits not only to **start** a conversation, but also to introduce new ideas **during** a conversation. So, we may wish to get someone's attention by saying, *Excuse me, please,* or we may wish to introduce a surprising piece of news with, *You may not believe this, but . . .*

Or we may want to add a small piece of information with, *By the way . . .* Something more serious can be introduced with, *In my view.* If you try to use the gambits in this section in the activities as much as you can, you will remember them more easily when you have real conversations outside the classroom.

1. Asking for Information

You want to buy the things below. What would you say to the shop assistant? Use suitable phrases from the list.

THE SHOP ASSISTANT	YOU
May I help you?	electric typewriter — price? (*Example: Yes, I'd like to know how much this typewriter costs.*)
What can I do for you?	bicycle — how many gears?
Yes?	desk lamp — what kind of bulb it takes?
Would you like some help?	these pyjamas — different colours?
What would you like?	stereo receivers — which is the best?
Can I help you?	oil — which is the best for my car?
Are you looking for something?	batteries — where in the supermarket?
Do you need help?	shampoo — for **my** hair?
You look lost.	a carrier bag — how much and where?

I'd like to know . . .

I'm interested in . . .

Could you tell me . . . ?

Do you know . . . ?

Could you find out . . . ?

Could I ask . . . ?

¹Do you happen to know . . . ?

1. Less likely the assistant will know.

8

[1]**Excuse me**

Sorry

Excuse me for interrupting, but . . .

May I interrupt for a moment?

. . ., [2]please

[3]**Certainly**

---

2. Breaking in

Often we have to approach strangers to ask them for some information or help.

Two to four students volunteer to be the questioners. They should think up some things to ask about (ideas below).

The rest of the class stand up and form small groups (3/4) and talk about anything you want. (hobby? friend? tomorrow? holiday?)

The volunteers then approach the groups and 'break in' to ask their questions. Try to use phrases from the list.

When each of the volunteers has been to each of the groups, everybody sits down again. The volunteers then report the answers they got.

Examples

Excuse me, can you tell me how to get to the cafeteria?

May I interrupt for a moment? I'd like to know how to get to the cafeteria.

Some things to ask about

How to get to the nearest supermarket/bus stop/telephone box.
Where you can get change/a haircut/stamps.
Where you could find a good, but not too expensive restaurant.
Where to get advice on buying a computer/new car.

---

1. Used to attract attention.

2. Most common at the end of a request.

3. The friendly way to say Yes.

3. Interrupting Game

The teacher (or a student volunteer) chooses a topic and starts to talk about it. Anyone in the class then tries to interrupt, using one of the phrases in the list.

The speaker answers, but after that brings the discussion back to the original topic.

Try to interrupt as often as possible and in different ways.

Example

— **Last night I went to a football match . . .**
— **Excuse me for interrupting, but which one?**
— **Arsenal against Liverpool.**
— **Anyway, so I went to the game, got my seat . . .**
— **Sorry, but where exactly were you sitting?**
— **In the main stand. As I was saying, I . . .**

Some possible topics

1. What you did last night
2. A funny thing that happened at work
3. A joke you heard recently
4. An argument you've had with someone
5. How you get to work or school
6. A fabulous meal you've enjoyed recently

Sorry, but . . .

Excuse me for interrupting, but . . .

Can I add here that . . .

I'd like to comment on that.

Can I add something?

Can I say something here?

I'd like to say something, if I may.

Can I ask a question?

¹May I ask something?

To return to the topic

Anyway, . . .

In any case, . . .

To get back to what I was saying, . . .

Where was I?

1. Some people think *may* is more polite than *can* in questions like this.

I'm calling to find out . . .

I'd like to ask . . .

Could you tell me . . .

I'm calling about . . .

I was wondering if you could tell me . . .

I wonder if you could help me . . .

If you go through a switchboard, say first:

I'd like to talk to somebody about . . .

4. Getting Information on the Phone

Asking a complicated question is difficult. Asking it on the phone is even more difficult.

Work in pairs. Section 1 gives you the information you need to ask your questions; Section 2 gives the answers. Match up the information with the correct answer. Then take turns to ask the questions. You must start your questions with one of the phrases from the list.

Section 1

1. You are calling the theatre to find out what time this evening's performance starts.

2. You are calling the post office to find out how to send a parcel to New Zealand so that it arrives in time for Christmas.

3. You are ringing the airline to find out the earliest flight from Tokyo to Hong Kong a week tomorrow.

4. You are ringing your doctor's surgery to make an appointment with Dr Crawford.

5. You are ringing your local paper to find out how to place an advertisement — you want to sell a pair of skis.

6. You are ringing Snodgrass and White, a local firm of solicitors, to find out about their job advertisement in your local paper.

7. You are ringing a language school to find out how much their evening courses cost.

8. You are ringing the local railway station to find out if trains are running normally again after yesterday's storm.

Section 2

a. Part-time/£60 per week/secretary/telephonist.

b. By surface before Nov 1st/By air before Dec 3rd.

c. All running approx. 20 minutes late/no buffet services available.

d. It has been cancelled.

e. Ads must be placed by 4.30 pm on day prior to day of issue/pay cash at the office or credit card by phone.

f. Two evenings/three hours per evening/£60 per term; four evenings/three hours per evening/£120 per term.

g. 6.30 am (then 10.30, 15.30, 19.00).

h. He is on holiday for a month/his assistant is Dr Mills.

5. Actions in Order

Activity 1

Here are some rules from an instruction manual on how to catch a shoplifter. The order of the instructions is mixed up. You are the manager, training a new store detective. What would you say to the trainee. Use phrases from the list. First re-order the instructions.

○ The detective asks the shoplifter to come to the manager's office.

○ The detective acts as if (s)he were buying something.

○ The detective waits until the shoplifter has gone out of the store before stopping him or her.

○ When the detective sees a shoplifter taking something, (s)he does not show that (s)he has noticed.

○ The detective simply taps the shoplifter on the shoulder and says, "I think you have something that isn't yours".

○ The detective dresses as (s)he normally would to go shopping.

Activity 2

The following are some basic rules to follow if your photocopier refuses to work. The order in which to apply these rules is mixed up. Imagine you are showing a new employee what to do when the machine does not work. Re-order the rules and introduce them with phrases from the list.

○ Do not try to repair the machine yourself.

○ Press the re-start button before closing the cabinet.

○ Check that there is paper in the paper-feed tray.

○ Check the toner (black ink) level. Replace if empty.

○ Call the engineer if the machine is still not working.

○ Check that there is no paper jammed between the rollers.

○ Do not use a screwdriver or any other metal tool. You could easily electrocute yourself.

First of all,

Then,

Next,

After that,

Finally,

Make sure you . . .

Be careful not to . . .

Remember to . . .

Don't forget to . . .

12

First,

First of all,

To begin with,

Then,

After that,

So,

So then,

At the end,

Finally,

The sketches below show a bank robbery.

If you are in class —
Make up a story where each student introduces one step of the story using a suitable phrase from the list.

If you are working alone — write out the story in such a way that it could be read on the radio.

Some additional vocabulary is given at the bottom of the page. If you are unsure of the meaning of a word, check in a dictionary.

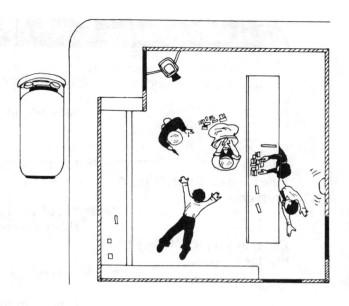

Additional vocabulary

Nouns: robbers, hoods, balaclavas, van, bag, gun, manager, bank clerk, counter, bundles, notes, alarm, closed-circuit television

Verbs: park, rush, threaten, hold, fill, count, terrify, lie, hand over, make a getaway, run, start the engine.

First of all, . . .

The main reason is . . .

Secondly, . . .

with two:

The other reason is . . .

with several:

Another reason is . . .

Besides that,

And on top of that,

And finally,

7. Listing Excuses

Here is a telephone conversation explaining why you can't go on a weekend trip with friends as you had planned. Fill in the phrases from the list.

You   **Your friend**

Hello?

Hi, this is Bob. How are you?

Fine thanks. What's the problem?

I'm afraid I can't go with you this weekend.

Oh, that's a pity. What's the matter?

Two things actually . . . _____ my brother is in town for the weekend, and _____ I'm afraid I'm a bit short of money at the moment.

Writing

Write down some more reasons why you can't go on the trip. Start each with a phrase from the list. Then list them in order of importance.

Speaking

1. Make up some other reasons for not going.
   Present them quickly in order of importance to another student.

2. Work in pairs, taking turns to invite and find excuses for turning down invitations to:
   a. go out to a really expensive restaurant tonight

   b. spend a fortnight — not a week — cycling in the country this summer

   c. come round to your home to see your huge collection of butterflies

You will find it easier if you make a short note of your excuses before you start.

8. The Main Thing

What do you look for in a job — good money, a challenge, the freedom to be creative, a chance to work with people?

Speaking

Work in pairs. Write down what you think is the most important thing about a job. Tell your partner, and then (s)he reports it to the class. Try to use the phrases in the list.

Example

To your partner:
I think the most important thing is a lot of money.

To the class:
Marie thinks the most important thing is earning a lot of money.

Writing

Write your answers. What do you look for when you apply for a job?

Discussion

Try to use the phrases when you talk about the following:

1. The most important thing to look for in a future boy/girlfriend/ wife/husband.

2. What is important when bringing up a child?

3. You are planning a walking holiday in the mountains. How should you prepare?

4. You are driving along an icy road when suddenly the car starts to skid.

5. You are going for a very important interview. You are usually so nervous at interviews that you do badly. How should you prepare this time?

First of all,

The main thing is . . .

The most important thing is . . .

The trouble is . . .

The problem is . . .

The real problem is . . .

The point is . . .

The [1]awful thing is . . .

Don't forget that . . .

9. The Main Problem

Divide into two teams. The students in one team pick one of the topics from Column A.

A member of the other team has to say a related sentence from Column B, starting with a phrase from the list — within 15 seconds.

Some of the sentences in column B fit more than one topic — or none at all! If in doubt, ask the players to explain any choices you don't understand.

Example

| Highjackers | **The trouble is, nobody knows how to handle them.** |

Round 1

A	B
Raising children	It makes saving a waste of time.
The rising cost of living	Nobody knows how to handle it.
Learning a language on your own	It's an uphill struggle.
Living together	The further away you are, the worse it is.

Round 2

A	B
Television	It wears you out before the day is over.
Mother-in-law for the weekend	Nobody knows how to handle it.
	It makes you feel so depressed.
Jogging	It bores you to tears.
Smoking	Everybody gets on everybody's nerves.
	You need will-power to stop.

Round 3

Try again. This time the topics are given, the other team has to make up a suitable response using one of the phrases.

Topics. Drugs, football hooligans, unemployment, famine, forgetting to do your homework, flying, computers, politics, learning English.

1. Alternatives to *awful* are *terrible*, *worst*.

10. A Surprising Fact

Speaking

Sometimes the best way to support an argument is to come up with an unexpected fact.

The following paragraph contains some surprising facts (given in *italics*).

Read the paragraph aloud and introduce each of these facts with one of the phrases from the top list, and add a qualifier from the bottom list.

Example

TV plays a very large part in British life. (There were 2.3 TV's per household in Britain in 1987.)

— **Do you realize that there were, on average, 2.3 TV's per household in Britain in 1987? Normally TV is an important part of British life.**

> **TV has a tremendous effect on children.** (*Children spend more time watching TV than doing anything else in their waking hours.*) Early in life, children learn from TV to influence their parents about what to buy — not just in the area of toys, but also at the supermarket. (*Women buy more snack foods when accompanied by children.*) Also, when parents don't limit their children's TV watching, they become so dependent on television for their entertainment that they begin to lose their potential for creativity. (*A study has shown that children without TV who are left to themselves develop their own creative powers.*) Many people are also worried about the high percentage of programmes that highlight violence. (*Children have been shown to learn violence from TV.*) In short, the negative effects of TV probably outweigh its possible positive influence in presenting the world to the growing child.

Writing

Write out the sentences in italics — each with its opening phrase and its qualifier.

Discussion

Do you agree with the text you read?
If not, give your arguments and try to include some surprising facts which you know.

Start:

Do you realise that . . .

Believe it or not,

You may not believe it, but . . .

It may sound strange, but . . .

[1]The surprising thing is . . .

[1]Surprisingly,

[2]Oddly enough,

[2]Funnily enough,

End with:

Generally

By and large

As a rule

Normally

Usually

On the whole,

1. These relate to a point you have already made — they come in the middle of what you are saying.

2. These connect what you say to what has just been said — usually they introduce a *coincidence*.
All of these expressions are rather informal, and will sound natural used to somebody you know rather well.

Guess what!

Surprise!

I've got news for you!

Do you know what!

Are you sitting down?

You'd better sit down!

You won't believe this, but . . .

11. Surprising News

Writing

Write brief dialogues describing some good and bad things that have happened (or will happen) to you. Use the phrases in the list.

Example

Guess what! I found that five pound note you that lost last month!

— Did you! where was it?

Surprise! It was in the pocket of the jeans you lent me!

1. _____ We don't have any classes today!

2. _____ I know who's come first in the class!

3. _____ Have you heard our teacher's getting married?

4. Now write a dialogue with your own surprising news.

Speaking

First, each student tries to think of some good and bad news. Make a list.

Each student then takes his turn presenting the news to the class. Remember to use the phrases in the list.

Good News	Bad News
_____	_____
_____	_____
_____	_____
_____	_____
_____	_____

12. An Unpleasant Thought

Yesterday you were invited to see the new home of a friend. You were not very impressed by it. In fact, everything that (s)he thought was wonderful, you didn't like.

Writing

Re-write these ideas using the phrases in the list to introduce your ideas:

1. She thought it was very spacious, but you felt the ceilings were too low.

2. She had bought most of her furniture second-hand, and you thought it looked cheap and rather old-fashioned.

3. She was very proud of her choice of wallpaper, but you thought it made the whole place look dark.

4. She thought the view from the balcony was fantastic, but all you could see was the tops of other houses.

5. She was especially pleased with the coffee table which her husband had made. You thought it looked rough and not very well made.

6. On the coffee table there was a lamp which she said she had paid £200 for. She said it was 18th century and worth a lot more. You saw the same ones on sale for £25 in a local store.

Speaking

Write down some more possible ideas, then act them out in front of the class.

_____

_____

_____

_____

_____

_____

_____

Actually,

The only thing is . . .

To tell you the truth,

To be honest,

¹Frankly,

1. This expression is the one you would most often use to introduce something you knew would annoy or insult the other person. It can be a real warning of a shock to come!

20

Frankly, I doubt if . . .

Let's face it,

The catch is . . .

The truth of the matter
is . . .

The real question is . . .

[1]Come on now!

Let's be realistic.

1. Used only with friends.

13. The Hidden Truth

Study this advertisement for a French course that claims it is better than all other courses.

★ ★ ★ ★ ★ ★ ★ ★ ★ ★ ★ ★ ★ ★ ★ ★ ★

Learn to speak and think in French in 10 easy lessons!

by F. L. Murphy
Chairman of French Quick Ltd.

Aren't you surprised at how quickly a child learns a language? We, at French Quick Ltd, have studied how children learn and we have produced a course that's second to none and makes learning French as easy as child's play!
No need to learn all those boring lists of irregular verbs or pages and pages of dull vocabulary. We guarantee you'll be speaking French like a Parisian in just 10 lessons.

Our new revolutionary approach — "Exclusive Submersion" — with the aid of video, and programmed lessons on computer, teaches you how to think and speak in French! You may ask, "How long will this take?" Well, not as long as you think. In just 10 lessons using the famous "Exclusive Submersion" method, we provide you with a vocabulary equal to that of the average native speaker of French, and you don't get a headache in the process!

The programmes are delivered to your door in carefully designed modules which you can work at in the comfort of your own home and at your own speed.

You'll be speaking French right from the very first lesson! And after only 10 lessons you'll be able to take part in any French conversation!

So don't waste another day! Write to me personally today, and I'll send you a free demonstration lesson.

Professor F. L. Murphy
French Quick Ltd.
The French Academy
36 Cottage Lane
Avon by Sea

★ ★ ★ ★ ★ ★ ★ ★ ★ ★ ★ ★ ★ ★ ★ ★ ★

Speaking

In small groups, pick out sections of the advertisement which you find questionable. Discuss them using the phrases in the list.

For example:

"He says here, 'in just 10 lessons'. The catch is, how long is each lesson?"

Writing

Write a complaint to the newspaper about the advertisement. Use the phrases from the list. You may find phrases from the following list helpful as well.

It's not fair to say . . .
It's deceptive to say . . .
He makes useless promises.
A typical sales technique.
Money-back guarantee.

22

Talking of . . .

That reminds me . . .

[1]By the way,

Oh, before I forget, . . .

14. Changing the Subject

Work in small groups — minimum 4, maximum 10. Sit in a circle. One person starts by saying the first thing that comes to mind about last weekend.

For example: **I didn't get much work done last weekend.**
The next person changes the subject using a phrase from the list:
Talking of weekends, we're thinking of having a party next weekend.

Continue till all the ideas are finished, then start again with your own ideas.
If someone cannot say something, they drop out of the game. The winner is the person left when everyone else has dropped out.

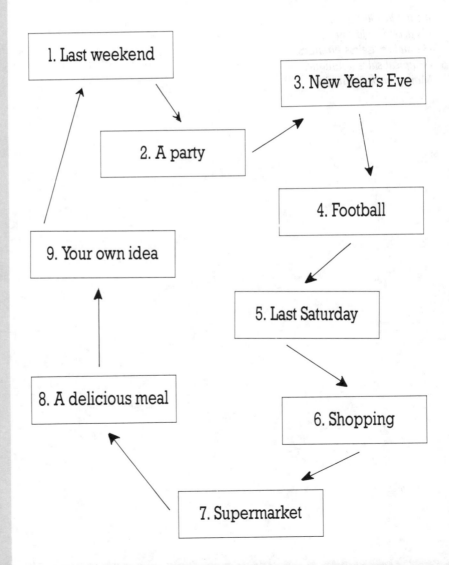

---

1. This is also used to "interrupt yourself", when you remember something you want to tell the other person and digress on to it.

15. Current Affairs

Preparation

Listen to today's news or buy today's newspaper. Pick a news item which you are interested in — perhaps something you know a little about. Write short notes giving your opinion of the news item.

(If you cannot listen to the news or buy a paper, there is a list of possible topics at the bottom of this page).

When everyone has prepared their opinions, work in groups of 3 or 4. Each student then states his or her opinion using the phrases from the list.

Writing

After making the short notes, students may then write out their opinions in full sentences as if they were writing an article for a students' magazine or 'leader' article for a newspaper.

Alternative news items

1. A recent report suggests that work is playing too important a role in people's lives.

2. A survey has just been published showing that only 2% of the population go to church regularly. Is religion less meaningful today?

3. After a series of horrific killings, the government is trying to ban guns completely from private use. Only the army and police would be allowed to carry guns.

4. The Education Secretary announced last week that he is thinking of lowering the school leaving age from 16 to 13 so that young people who do not like school can leave for a couple of years, get a job, then come back later in life.

5. The Government of an African republic has announced that it now has nuclear weapons. It has thousands of starving and homeless people in parts of the country away from the capital.

I think . . .

I suppose . . .

I ¹suspect that . . .

I'm ²pretty sure that . . .

I'm fairly certain that . . .

It's my opinion that . . .

I'm ³convinced that . . .

I ⁴wonder if . . .

1. Gives a tentative opinion.

2. Informal, only with friends.

3. A strong opinion.

4. A way of giving an "open" opinion, which invites other people to comment too.

I'd say . . .

Could it be . . .

Perhaps it's . . .

I think it's . . .

It looks like . . .

It's difficult to say, but I'd guess . . .

16. Guessing

Work in groups of 3 or 4. Take it in turns to guess the answers to the questions. Do not think about your answers. Just try to guess and use the phrases in the list.

1. What do the following pictures show?

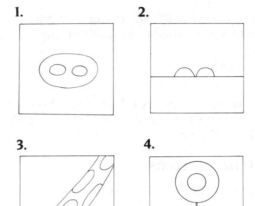

2. How long is this line?

_____

3. How many dots are there in this heap?

5. Which of these two circles is larger?

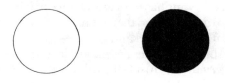

4. Which of these is the longer?

6. Each of these lines says, "I speak English".
In which language?

a. Ik praat engels.
b. Eu falo ingles.
c. Beszélek angolul.
d. Linguam anglicam loquor.

e. Jeg taler engelsk.
f. Eigo-ga dekimasu.
g. Ninasema kiingareza.
h. Ana kalam al inglise.

Possible choices
Sudanese, Dutch, Japanese, Hungarian, Latin, Swahili, Danish, Portuguese.

I'd say . . .

Could it be . . .

Perhaps it's . . .

I think it's . . .

It looks like . . .

It's difficult to say, but I'd guess . . .

I honestly feel that . . .

I [1]strongly believe that . .

I'm convinced that . . .

Without a doubt,

I'm positive . . .

I'm [2]absolutely certain that . . .

17. A Conviction

Read the following point of view. Decide whether you agree or not.

"I feel that everyone has the same chance in life. We're all born, go to school, and then we have a choice. Some people want to work hard and get on — they buy nice homes and big cars. Other people just laze around and never do very much. Just last week I was down in the centre of town and this long-haired guy came up to me and asked for money. I didn't give him any money, but I gave him a piece of advice. I told him to have his hair cut and get a job like everyone else. He just gave me a dirty look and walked away. He'll get nowhere in life with an attitude like that. But if he worked hard like me, he could have everything I have."

Writing

1. If you agree, write 10 sentences saying why. Use the ideas in the text and the phrases in the list.
2. If you disagree, write 10 sentences explaining why. You may want to mention the following ideas:

social class	quality of school
inflation	the individual
unemployment	

Speaking

Divide the class into those who agree and those who disagree. Discuss the different arguments in the two groups. Each group should decide on one person to present the main arguments. After these two people have spoken, everyone should join in the discussion.

Topics for further discussion:

Drinking and driving
Apartheid in South Africa
Nuclear energy
Money spent on Space Research

1. Alternative *firmly.*

2. Very strong.

18. Personal Opinions

You have been stopped in the street by a lady conducting an opinion poll. You think she is trying to sell you something, but she works for a national newspaper and is trying to find out about modern attitudes.

Work in pairs — one person asks the questions. When all the pairs have finished, change partners. The people who asked the questions must now answer.

Use the phrases in the list to introduce your opinions.

---

1. Who should be the boss in a family — the man or the woman?
2. Who ought to do the cooking — the man or the woman?
3. Who ought to do the dishes?
4. Who ought to fix things when they are broken?
5. Who ought to wash the clothes?
6. Who ought to be the one earning the most money?
7. Who ought to look after the children when they are under five years old?
8. Who ought to buy the clothes for the children when they are under 10 years old?
9. Who ought to discipline the children when they're naughty?
10. Who ought to pay the bills and organise the family's finances?

Discussion

What about your own up-bringing. How did your parents split the work in the home?

In some homes, the wife earns more than the husband. Should the husband give up work to look after the children, and let the woman be the breadwinner?

Remember to practise the phrases!

In my [1] opinion,

I personally believe . . .

I personally think . . .

I personally feel . . .

Not everyone will agree with me, but . . .

To [2] my mind, . . .

1. Stronger if you add *personal*.

2. Stress *my;* can sound rather dogmatic or opinionated.

28

In my opinion,

From my point of view,

Well, personally,

If I had ¹my way,

What ¹I'm more concerned with is . . .

In ¹ my case

19. How something affects you

Think of all the changes you would like to make in your classroom routine. For example, you may wish to change the times of your classes, have longer holidays, have smaller classes etc.

Speaking

In pairs, one student propose a change. The second student should explain how this would affect him or her personally.

Example

Student 1: **Why don't we come to school in the afternoons and evenings. I hate coming to school in the morning.**

Student 2: **Well, from my point of view that's impossible. The only bus I can get is in the morning. There are no buses around lunchtime.**

Writing

Each student writes down a proposed change on a piece of paper. Students pass their papers to another student who writes down an objection.

Ideas for changes

Why don't we spend more time talking?
I'd like to have more breaks.
I'd like to do some more grammar exercises.
Can we read English newspapers for a change?

1. Stress *my*, or *I*,

20. Sharing a Confidence

Speaking

Start a rumour about someone you know by whispering it to your neighbour. Use one of the phrases from the list. The neighbour can pass the rumour on or add something to it to make it more interesting. Continue until the rumour has gone round the whole class. The last person announces it to the whole class.

This activity will only work if **the rumours are not true.** If anyone tries to be nasty to someone, the game **must be stopped** and re-started.

Writing

Circulate rumours on paper. Everyone starts a rumour about his neighbour to the left. Write it at the top of a sheet of paper. Everyone then passes his piece of paper to the person on his right. Change the rumour a little and start it with one of the phrases from the list. Fold over the first rumour so that the next person can see only the latest rumour. Pass the paper on, each person changing the rumour. When the rumours have gone round the class and reached the person they are about that person reads the last rumour on the sheet.

Possible rumours

has fallen in love with a famous film star
has won a lot of money in a lottery
has just bought a VERY expensive car
is going to emigrate to New Zealand
might be promoted

I've heard . . .

[1] They say . . .

Just between you and me,

I heard [2] on the grapevine

This shouldn't be passed around, but . . .

Have you heard . . .

Maybe I shouldn't say this, but . . .

1. Often used to introduce rumours about public matters, what the Government is going to do etc.

2. *On the grapevine* means "from other people, in general office talk".

Why not . . .

Why don't you . . .

You could always . . .

One way would be to . . .

Perhaps you could . . .

If I were you, I'd . . .

What about . . . ing.

Try . . . ing.

21. How to get the Money

Write down 10 ways of getting money

1. _____   6. _____
2. _____   7. _____
3. _____   8. _____
4. _____   9. _____
5. _____   10. _____

Speaking

In pairs one student reads a problem. The other suggests a way of getting the money to solve the problem.

1. "I want to find another flat. My neighbours make so much noise I can't sleep. I've found a really nice place, but they want £1000 as a deposit."

2. I've just seen the car of my dreams. It's a 1960 Ford, but it's in perfect condition. The owner is leaving for Australia tomorrow and wants £800 cash. What can I do?"

3. "They've got a sale on in the electricity showroom. There's this super vacuum for £50. It normally costs £90. The trouble is I've only got £35 on me. If I don't go back down, it'll have gone."

4. Think of something you would really like to have. Decide its price. Ask your partner what you should do.

Writing

Write your problem on a piece of paper and pass it to your neighbour to suggest a solution.

22. Offering a Suggestion

Speaking

Think of how you could solve the problems below. Work in pairs taking turns to suggest solutions. Use the phrases in the list.

Problems

1. Some friends have come for dinner. You have pushed the cork into the wine bottle and people are waiting.
2. You have just locked your car door and realised that you have left the keys inside.
3. You and your friends have just been shopping and you're returning to the multi-storey car park. But you have forgotten where you left your car.
4. Every morning you turn off the alarm, go to sleep for another hour, and then you're late for work. You might lose your job.
5. You have just arrived at the airport and realise that you have left your plane ticket at home.
6. You invited one of your best friends for a meal yesterday evening, but she said she would be too busy at work. So you decided to go out alone. You saw her with another friend going into the cinema.
7. You had a test this morning in English. You saw a friend cheating. You don't know whether to speak to him about it.
8. Think of a problem you have or have had. Ask your partner to suggest a solution.

Writing

Write suggestions to each of the problems above.

Why don't you . . .

Why not . . .

Perhaps you could . . .

Have you thought about . . .

I have an idea

[1]Let's . . .

---

1. Only used to suggest doing something *together*.

Our plan is to . . .

We're thinking of . . .

What we have in mind
is . . .

What we plan to do is . . .

I'll tell you what we'll do.

What about this for an
idea . . .

23. The Great Escape

You and three friends have been put in prison in a far away country
for a crime you did not commit. Below you will find:
  a floor plan of the prison
  a map of that part of town
  the daily prison timetable
Work in groups of 4 to plan your escape.
Use the phrases from the list.

Speaking

Make your plan in note form and then present it to the class.

Writing

Write your plan in a letter to a friend who can help you escape from
the outside.

Prison timetable

8.00am	breakfast in the common dining-hall
9.00am	clean-up of cells
10.00am —	visiting hour: speaking is only
11.00am	permitted through the iron bars of the small cell door windows
12.00am	lunch in the cell
1.00pm	change of guards
2.00pm —	exercises for prisoners in the fenced-in
2.30pm	yard
6.00pm	dinner in the common dining hall
10.00pm	lights out

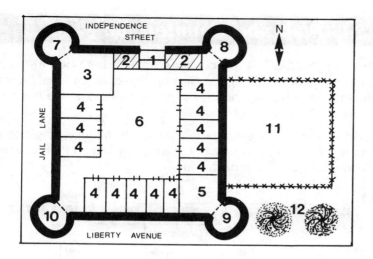

Floor plan

1 triple gate
2 guard rooms
3 guard common room
4 cells
5 common dining room
6 hall

7 northwest guard tower
8 northeast guard tower
9 southeast guard tower
10 southwest guard tower
11 fenced-in yard
12 trees along Liberty Avenue

Map of the town

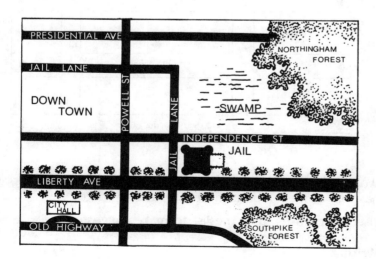

Why don't you . . .

You could always . . .

If I were you, I'd . . .

Why not . . .

How about . . .

Try   . . . ing .

24. Plan and Counterplan

It is 5.30 pm. Mark is at Francine's home where he's just had a snack. He has a lot of luggage. His train leaves at 5.45 pm. Francine offers to drive him to the railway station because she has to go out to the supermarket anyway.

Francine and Mark get into the car with 10 minutes to get to the station. It's only a short way, but more complicated than you think — especially at that time of day.

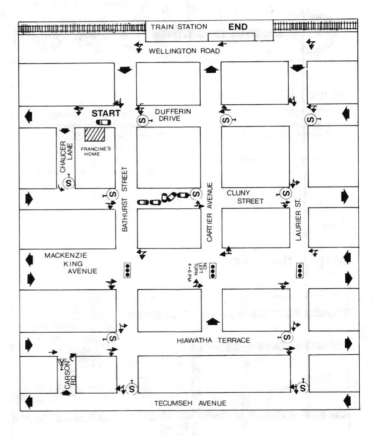

Work in pairs as the driver, Francine, and the helpful Mark, who has lots of ideas about the best possible route.

Use the phrases from the list to make suggestions

Writing

When you have finished and have arrived at the station, write out directions for the quickest possible route a) by car b) on foot.

2. Linking Gambits

Conversation is like a game of football. One player can only run with the ball in one direction for a certain time. Sooner or later he must change direction or pass the ball to another player. In a typical conversation, we can only talk about the same topic for a short time. Then we must move in a different direction, or give someone else a chance.

For example, we can link our own idea to what someone has just said with, *But the problem with that is* . . . or *Not to mention the fact that* . . . Sometimes it can be very difficult to say what you mean. You want another chance in the conversation, so you say, *Let me put it another way*. Or you may want to disagree, but in a way that will not offend with, *That's a good idea but* . . .

The main reason for using linking gambits is that your listeners will be more prepared for your arguments and views. They will know from your links whether you are going to agree or disagree. If you use links, you will find that you are more easily understood. Remember that a lot of the misunderstanding between people comes from *how* they say something, not *what* they say.

In a case like this,

In a situation like this,

In this sort of situation,

25. *Thinking about a Problem*

Here are two 'case studies' adapted from real life situations. Read through each one, think up a solution, and make a note on a piece of paper.

Speaking

Work in small groups. One student should ask for comments, and the other(s) offer a solution, trying to use the phrases in the list.

Writing

From your first notes, write a paragraph giving your solution.

Case 1

Frank has a good job in London working in the Department of the Environment. He has been in the same department since he left university and now he has special responsibility for Historic Buildings. If he stays there, he expects to be head of his department within 10 years. Cathy, his wife, has a very well-paid job with an insurance company based in the centre of London. She has been with the same firm for 12 years. The Government has decided to de-centralise Frank's department in order to create more jobs in the North of England. The department is moving to Newcastle. Frank and Cathy have two children who are very happy in their schools. They have lots of friends. It would be impossible for Cathy to get such a good job in Newcastle. Frank wants to become head of his department. What should the family do?

Case 2

Yung-ae is from Korea. She's the mother of three children (3, 5 and 9). The youngest was born in Britain, but the others were born in Korea. Recently, the two older children have been giving her a lot of trouble. When she speaks to them in Korean, they answer her in English, and they speak English to each other. When the family goes out together, they pretend that they are not part of it. When they bring friends home, they get very embarrassed when Yung-ae speaks to them in Korean. They have become very cheeky to both their father and their mother. What can Yung-ae do?

26. Emphasising a Point

Read through this case study. Write answers to the questions which follow. Then work in pairs and groups to act out the role play situations. Try to use the phrases from the list.

Case Study

Edward and Adrienne are students at a London polytechnic. They have known each other for two years and have been going out together for 18 months. They are very serious about their relationship. They are thinking about getting married when they leave college in a year's time. Edward is English and comes from a middle class background. His parents live in Carlisle in the north of England. Adrienne is black and is on a scholarship from her home in Zimbabwe. They both realise the problems of a mixed marriage. And, of course, there are many cultural differences. They are young, tolerant, and they help each other in their studies. Edward's parents knew he had a girlfriend, but had not met Adrienne until last week. Edward had not told them that she was black. The parents were very polite and they seemed to get on well with Adrienne. Later, Adrienne said that she thought Edward's parents seemed disappointed she was not white. Edward knew what she meant and couldn't help feeling hurt and disappointed that his parents were not more enthusiastic.

Questions

1. What do you think is Edward's biggest worry?
2. What problems would Adrienne face if she married Edward?
3. What problems would Edward face?
4. What do Edward's parents probably think of the situation?
5. How do you think Adrienne's parents will feel if she marries in England?

Role-play situations

Prepare, then act out the following situations. Try to use the phrases in the list.

1. Edward talking to his best friend.
2. Adrienne talking to her best friend.
3. Edward's parents talking about the situation alone.
4. Edward's parents talking to their best friends.

That's just the point.

But the question is . . .

But the real question is . . .

This raises the problem of . . .

But can't you see . . .

To start with,

And another thing,

What's more,

Just a small point,

Perhaps I should mention . . .

Oh, I almost forgot . . .

27. Adding Things

There has been a particularly brutal murder in your town. Last night the police put out a picture of a man they would like to question. You have just been in town shopping and you are sure you saw the man. You decide to go in to your nearest police station.

Speaking

Work in pairs with one student as policeman. Use the phrases in the list. You will find help with vocabulary to describe the man below.

Facial features

eyes:	*blue, brown, green, dark, grey*
complexion:	*light, fair, pale, tanned*
nose:	*long, narrow, flat, wide, hooked*
eyebrows:	*thick, thin*
glasses:	*heavy frames, metal frames, large round*
moustache:	*bushy, thin, small*
ears:	*large, small, pointed, sticking-out, pierced*
mouth:	*tight-lipped, large lips*
hair:	*short, curly, long, straight, straggly, parting, dirty, styled, blond, brown, black, grey, auburn*
other features:	*beard, sideburns, freckles, mole, scar, unshaven*

Variation

When you have described the wanted man above choose a famous person to describe. Can the others guess who you are describing?

Writing

Write a description of the man which you could give to the police.

28. Give a Reason

Sit in a circle. Take a piece of paper and write down a job that would suit the student to your *left*, and the reason for choosing that job. For example, if you think your neighbour would make a good taxi-driver, you can write, I *think you should be a taxi-driver, because you are such a careful driver.*

Fold the paper so that the next student cannot read what you have written, but put the name of the student to your left at the bottom of the paper. Then pass it to the student on your *right*.

This student adds a new reason for choosing a job. For example, he or she could add, A*nd besides, you're so popular with women.* Then pass the paper to the next student on the *right*.

Continue round the circle until each paper comes back to the student whose name is at the bottom of the page. At that point each student reads the list of suggestions to the rest of the class. Don't forget to use the important phrases.

Some reasons for choosing a job

1. This may be your last chance to make some money.
2. Think how famous you would be.
3. You seem to enjoy working with people.
4. Have you thought what it would do for your image?
5. Anything is an improvement on what you're doing now.

And besides,

Also,

[1]In addition,

What's more,

And another thing,

Not to mention the fact that . . .

Plus the fact that . . .

Not only [2]that, but . . .

1. More formal.

2. Stress *that*.

Starting

The reason why . . .

Because . . .

Continuing

Because of that . . .

That's why . . .

That's the reason why . . .

¹For this reason . . .

29. Have you got a Good Reason?

Write down four things which you should have done recently, but didn't. For example:

a letter you haven't yet written
a book you haven't returned
a person you haven't rung
a visit you haven't made

Speaking

Work in pairs. First, exchange lists of what you haven't done. One student should start to challenge the other. Start:

You should have . . .
You'll have to . . .
Why haven't you . . .

Answer with good reasons, using the phrases in the list to introduce your reasons.

Example

Problem: I haven't given you back the book I borrowed from you last summer.

Student 1: I only gave you that book for a short time. You should have given it back months ago.

Student 2: I'm sorry. The reason why I haven't given you it back is because I couldn't find it. I packed all my books in boxes when I moved; that's why I can't find anything at the moment.

1. More formal.

30. Thinking Ahead

The class sits in a circle. The first student connects two of the ideas in the bubbles below, using one of the linking words from the list.

For example:

> **If I lose my job, I'll have to sell the house.**

The next student now has five seconds to connect the second idea with another.

For example:

> **If I sell the house, I'll have to live with my mother.**

If you cannot think of a sentence, you must drop out of the game. When all the ideas have been used, you may think of your own. Continue the game until there is only one person left, of until the end of 10 minutes.

If . . .

If I ever . . .

When . . .

Whenever . . .

As soon as . . .

By the time . . .

Unless . . .

What I mean is . . .

What I meant was . . .

Let me put it another way.

What I'm saying is . . .

What I'm trying to say is . . .

Don't misunderstand me,

If I said that, I didn't mean to . . .

¹Let me rephrase what I just said.

31. Correcting Yourself

Sometimes we say something which we don't really mean. Then we must go back and say it again, but more clearly and more accurately.

Work with another student and make one of the statements in the list below. They are all rather extreme, so you should moderate what you say, using a phrase from the list.

For example:

Student 1: **I never learn anything in school.**
Student 2: **Do you really mean that?**
Student 1: **Well, what I mean is I don't think I learn very much — maybe from one or two teachers, but not all.**

Extreme statements

1. I can't stand teachers.
2. I'd never live in England.
3. I never swear.
4. People who smoke in public should be fined.
5. Students are lazy.
6. I always say exactly what I think.
7. I never have to look a word up in the dictionary.
8. I don't make grammar mistakes.

Now think of your own prejudices:

9. I hate _____.
10. I never _____.
11. People who _____ should be put in prison.
12. _____ shouldn't be allowed.

---

1. More formal.

32. Putting the Record Straight

Sometimes people have misunderstood us so badly that we have to 'put the record straight' and explain.

Speaking

Student 2 has done something — for a good reason, but this is not what Student 1 has heard.
Work in pairs. Student 1 starts and Student 2 should try to explain the truth using the information and a phrase from the list. Each student must only look at their own part.

Student 1 starts:

1. What's this I heard about you jogging because you were getting fat?
2. Someone said to me that you've gone on a diet so that you won't have to buy new clothes.
3. I heard you're learning Spanish so that you can visit your girlfriend in Madrid.
4. What's this I heard about you cycling to work because you can't afford the petrol for your car?
5. Someone told me you're thinking of giving up English lessons because you think you'll never learn.

Student 2 — The Truth

1. You decided to start jogging in order to keep fit.
2. You have gone on a diet because your doctor told you to. You have a serious health problem and you have no choice about dieting.
3. You are learning Italian in order to go on holiday there in the summer. You do not have a Spanish girlfriend.
4. You have recently started cycling to work in an attempt to keep fit.
5. You think you may have to stop coming to English lessons because you are too busy to spare the time.

That's not what I said at all.

I've no idea who told you that.

Goodness, where did you get that idea from?

[1]I'm afraid that just isn't true.

The fact of the matter is . . .

[2]Look, let's get this straight, . . .

1. Much stronger without *I'm afraid.*

2. Shows not only that you've been misunderstood, but you are annoyed about it.

Introducing

Many people think . . .

Some people say . . .

You've probably heard that . . .

It may seem . . .

Linking

But in fact,

But actually,

The truth of the matter is . . .

33. *Popular Misconceptions*

Speaking

Just because many people believe something does not make it true. Work in pairs with the popular misconceptions below. Take it in turns to explain what is wrong with the statement. First state the 'myth' using one of the introductions in the list, then give the truth using one of the linking phrases.

For example

Many people think that lightning never strikes twice in the same place, but actually it often does.

Misconceptions

1. Columbus discovered America.
2. Men can stand greater pain than women.
3. Eating red meat makes you aggressive.
4. Oysters make you sexier.
5. If you touch a frog or toad, you'll get warts.
6. Bats are blind.
7. Flying is always faster than taking the train.
8. If you get hiccups, hold your breath and count to ten.
9. If you burn you skin, put butter on it.
10. If you get your feet wet, you'll get a cold.

Think of similar ideas which you have heard and discuss the truth in pairs.

Writing

Write out each misconception and explanation.

34. We take it for Granted

When we look at a glass of clean water, we think that the water is pure and clean. But if we look at a drop of the same water under a microscope, we may discover that it is full of things which are invisible to the naked eye. We could say:

At first glance it looks as if this is a glass of clean water. But in fact, if we look at it under a microscope, we see all kinds of things.

Work in pairs and work out descriptions of the following pairs of pictures.

1.

2.

3.

Describe the following in a similar way:

4. The surface of your skin
5. The hospital service
6. The police
7. Unemployed people
8. Teachers in city schools
9. The social services
10. Yourself

At first glance it looks as if . . .

Many people think that . . .

We take it for granted that . . .

It seems as if . . .

It looks like . . .

But in fact,

In reality,

The fact of the matter is . . .

But actually,

35. Saying 'no' Tactfully

If someone asks you to do something, you can say 'no' in a direct way or you can suggest doing something else.

In order to practise the phrases used to say no, students should work in pairs.

Each situation has the ideas for a dialogue where B says 'no' to what A is suggesting. Read only your own part, and use the phrases from the list.

Saying no

I'm not keen on . . .

I don't particularly like . .

I can't 'stand . . .

It's not my idea of . . .

I'd really rather not . . .

A preference

I'd ²prefer . . .

I'd really much rather . . .

I'd rather . . .

A

1. **Let's go out for dinner.**
   (You love going out to a hamburger bar, ordering everything, then eating it in your car.)
2. **Let's go to a concert.**
   (You want to go to a Bach concert. It will last 4 hours)
3. **Let's go for a drink.**
   (Your idea of an evening out is to go down to the pub and spend the evening drinking.)
4. **Do you fancy going walking at the weekend?**
   (You like to set off at 6 on Saturday mornings for a whole day in the hills.)
5. **Would you like to come and meet my parents?**
   (You are very keen that your friend meets your parents. You think (s)he likes you very much.)

B

1. Whenever you eat out, you like to go to one of the most expensive restaurants in town. You would never dream of going near a hamburger 'joint'.
2. You hate classical music and think it is only for snobs. There is a rock concert on at the ice rink tomorrow.
3. You are only 16 and know that if your parents knew you had been out drinking, they would be very angry.
4. Your idea of a nice weekend is to do absolutely nothing. You would be prepared to go for a walk round town to look at shops.
5. You know that A would like your friendship to become more serious, but you have your eye on someone else. In fact, you are hoping to go out with this other person tomorrow.

1. Followed by a noun *(people who . . .) (waiting)*.

2. Followed by a noun *(tea)*, or *to +* verb *(to wait)*.

36. Door-to-door Salespeople

Divide the class in two groups — the salespeople and the customers.
The salespeople are going to try to sell their goods to the customers
and they in turn are going to say 'no' to everything.

Salespeople

Get together for 10 minutes and study all the things you have to sell.
Make up good arguments why the consumers should buy them.

Customers

Get together and collect reasons why you do not need all the articles
below.
Each salesperson should pick a customer and try to sell the product
— politely. The customer must reject if for good reasons. The
salesperson then moves on to another customer until they have tried
to sell something to everyone!

Articles

1. Kitchen gadgets
   a. an electric toaster
   b. an electric can opener
   c. an electric corkscrew

2. Beauty aids
   a. a cream to take lines away
   b. a cream to remove unwanted hair
   c. a spray to make your hair any colour you want

3. Housework aids
   a. a spray to polish wood
   b. a carpet shampooer
   c. the most powerful vacuum cleaner ever made

4. Gardening aids
   a. a plant food which will make flowers last for months
   b. a chemical to make your grass look really green
   c. a spray which will kill all insects

I'm not really interested in . . .

But I'm not worried about . . .

I've got no use for . . .

I'm perfectly happy with . . .

¹Can you explain why . . .

Do you mean to say . . .

I don't understand why . . .

Why is it that . . .

How come . . .

Does this mean . . .

37. Demanding Explanations

Sometimes we find ourselves in a situation where we have little control over what happens to us. For example, imagine you are flying to London, to catch a connection to New York. You get to London Heathrow and you have three hours to catch your connecting flight. But there is a strike of baggage handlers. There are thousands of people trying to get information but it is impossible. You cannot get any explanation for anything.

Eventually, after you have been waiting for 12 hours, a representative of the airline is prepared to tell you and your fellow travellers what they know.

Speaking

Work in pairs with the information below, one student is the passenger, the other is the airline official. Use the phrases in the list.

Information available

1. There will be no definite information on departure for another two hours.
2. No meal vouchers will be available.
3. The airline cannot accept responsibility for baggage.
4. The airline will not pay for any hotel bills.
5. There is only one young man on duty giving information.
6. The aircraft is available and waiting to go; the problem is no baggage can be touched.

Writing

At the end of your trip, write a letter of complaint to the Complaints Department, Customer Services, Air World.

1. All of these show you are annoyed, and can easily sound aggressive (but of course you may want to!).

38. Expressing your Reservations

When someone puts forward a plan which you don't agree with completely, you have to be able to express your doubts and your reservations.

Imagine the situation where someone in your family — perhaps your son or your wife — suggests the following changes in your life. Work in pairs: one suggests the changes, the other expresses reservations. Use the phrases in the list to introduce your reservations.

Change 1

For ten years you have rented the same two-bedroomed flat. You now have two children, a girl and a boy. They will soon need their own rooms. What about looking for a bigger house?

Change 2

All your life you've had trouble sleeping. Every night, at about 3 in the morning you wake up, go to the kitchen, make yourself a cup of tea, and read a book. You then go back to bed and waken up around 8.30. Your partner thinks you should see a doctor.

Change 3

You were brought up to be very polite, and never say what you really think of someone. Your son has just told you that you are a hypocrite. He wants you to start showing people what you really think of them.

Change 4

You have always been a 'big eater'. As a result you are no longer as thin as you used to be. Your partner suggests you go on a crash diet!

'I'm afraid . . .

I don't see how . . .

But the problem is . . .

Yes, but . . .

I doubt . . .

Possibly, but . . .

Yes, but the problem really is . . .

What I'm worried about is . . .

What bothers me is . . .

1. The general phrase for introducing any answer which your listener may think is "unhelpful".

Bearing in mind . . .

Considering . . .

If you remember . . .

Allowing for the fact
that . . .

When you consider
that . . .

*Responding to a
compliment*

Oh, thank you very
much.

That's very kind of you.

Do you really think so?

39. Taking things into Consideration

Nobody is perfect, and few of us are really good at anything. We usually have difficulties to take into consideration.

First, write down some of your achievements in the left hand column, and the difficulties you had in the right-hand column.
For example, perhaps you got a good mark in English, but you didn't have much time to spend working at home.

	Achievement	Difficulty
1.	_____	_____
2.	_____	_____
3.	_____	_____
4.	_____	_____
5.	_____	_____

Work in pairs with your own ideas and with the ideas below. Ask your partner what his achievements are, and compliment him/her taking into account their difficulties.

For example:

Student 1: **How good is your English?**
Student 2: **Well, I can understand the news on TV.**
Student 1: **That's excellent, bearing in mind you've only been learning for a couple of months.**
Student 2: **Thank you very much.**

Ideas to help

Achievement	Difficulty
6. I passed my driving test.	The test was held at the rush-hour.
7. I got to the class on time.	There was snow on the roads.
8. I finished my course at the University.	I've got 3 young children.
9. I invited Bill.	He was very rude to me last week.
10. Sheila's just got a job.	She has written over a hundred letters.
11.	....

40. Arguments and Counter-arguments

Very often, when we have a plan, someone has an objection or a reservation. We then have to think up a counter-argument to try to persuade them.

In this dialogue the husband is trying to persuade his wife that they need a cottage in the country.

Him: Why don't we buy a cottage in the country — somewhere we could go at weekends and for holidays. **(Plan)**

Her: That's a good idea, but don't you think the children will get bored — can't you hear them — not the cottage AGAIN this summer! **(Reservation)**

Him: That's probably true, but I think it would be nice for us, and after all, it won't be long before they'll want to go off with their own friends. **(Counter-argument)**

Work in pairs with these ideas using the phrases for reservations and counter-arguments.

1. A: take up skiiing
   B: don't have the time or money
   A: it would be fun, good exercise

2. A: buy a flat
   B: can't afford it
   A: cheaper than paying rent

3. A: fly to Moscow
   B: cheaper to go by train
   A: we'd lose a week of holiday just travelling, plus all the money on food

4. A: buy a new car — the old one's rusty
   B: we haven't finished paying for the old one
   A: the old one's dangerous

5. A: have a party
   B: the neighbours would object
   A: why not invite the neighbours

6. A: your plan
   B: your reservation
   A: your counter-argument

Reservation

Yes, but . . .

Yes, but don't forget . . .

That would be great, except . . .

That's a good idea, but . . .

Counter-arguments

Even so,

Even if that is so,

That may be so, but . . .

That's probably true, but . . .

Possibly, but . . .

On the other hand,

But then again,

Look at it this way,

Anyway,

Even so,

OK, but . . .

But [1] in the long run,

Very true, but . . .

To make up for it, . . .

41. Seeing the Good Side

Are you an optimist or a pessimist? This is an optimist's game!
The class divides into two teams. Take turns to make complaints,
starting with the ideas below. The other side must try to say something
positive.

For example:

Team 1: **Everything's so expensive nowadays, isn't it?**
Team 2: **Yes, but on the other hand, wages are much higher than
they used to be.**

Each team take it in turn to make statements and to answer. The
answers must be introduced by one of the phrases from the list.
Each team has 10 seconds to answer. Play two or three 'rounds' with
each round lasting 5 minutes.

1. It's been raining now every day this month.
2. This coffee is really strong.
3. English is very difficult.
4. Grammar is really boring.
5. I hate learning to spell.
6. I've put on 5 kilos since Christmas.
7. Volvos are very expensive.
8. You can't park anywhere around here!
9. It can be very cold in Norway in winter.
10. I can't understand Pierre's accent.
11. Bill is very mean with money.
12. Liz is always late.
13. Joan can't dance. She's awful, isn't she!
14. Children have too much money these days.
15. Schools are far too liberal.
16. Teachers aren't strict enough.
17. I hate starting school at 8 in the morning.
18. It's wrong that people get paid for giving their blood.

1. This means "if you think on a
longer time scale".

42. Generalising

We all have irritating habits — at least in the eyes of other people! Pick a partner — if possible of the opposite sex. Your partner has just suggested that you ought to get married. You don't think you are suitable. Use one of the excuses below — an irritating habit.

Use more and more of the habits to try to persuade your partner that marriage is not for you.

When your partner is persuaded, change roles. You can use the following ideas or your own. Use the words and phrases from the list.

Irritating habits

1. I sleep with the window wide open even in the middle of winter.
2. I sing very loudly in the bath.
3. I quite often don't go to bed till 3 or 4 in the morning.
4. I can't cook at all. I'm happy with a hamburger. I don't like foreign food.
5. I am very moody. When I get up I can be in a great mood, but by lunchtime I can be so depressed that I have to go to the doctor.
6. I love to listen to very loud rock music — so loud that I can feel the room shake.
7. I talk in my sleep.
8. I snore very loudly.
9. I like to keep my flat cool. My room is never more than 15°.
10. I don't have a bath very often.
11. I smoke in bed.
12. I seldom do the dishes. I just let them pile up.

Discussion

1. What is the secret of a good marriage?
2. Which habits would annoy YOU in someone else?
3. Which of YOUR habits would you try to stop if you got married?

Generalising

As a rule,

Generally,

Usually,

Frequent

Most of the time

Again and again

Time and again

Less frequent

Every so often

From time to time

Every now and then

Generalising

In general,

Generally speaking,

As a rule,

By and large,

In my experience,

In most cases,

Exceptions

There are exceptions, of course,

One exception is . . .

But what about . . .

But don't forget . . .

43. Exceptions

Divide the class into two groups — the optimists and the pessimists. Each group must make a 'typical' statement using the ideas below. The other group must make a 'typical' comment with an exception. The pessimists will make pessimistic comments and state pessimistic exceptions — the optimists, vice versa.

For example:

Pessimist: **In general, British winters are pretty cold and dismal.**
Optimist: **They certainly can be, but there are exceptions, of course. Winters in the south west can be very mild.**

Ideas to talk about:

British cars	German cars
Men	Women
Summers	Winters
Pop stars	Politicians

Pessimistic comments:

very depressing	stupid
unreliable	too expensive
never work hard	tell lies
can't be trusted	

Optimistic comments:

good value	dependable
exciting	warm
dry	friendly
hardworking	

Possible Exceptions

my car	my sister
my cousin	last year
my teacher	our Prime Minister

44. The Generalisation Game

Work in small groups of 3 or 4. Below you will find lists of topics. Your teacher will tell you which list is yours. You must think of as many generalisations with exceptions as possible in the time allowed. One person in your group should write them down. Another person can agree to read them out to the class. The group with the most generalisations is the winner. For example:

In general old people are very conservative. There are exceptions, of course. My own grandmother started jogging when she was 80.

Topic list 1
1. Grandparents
2. Teenagers
3. Millionaires
4. Teachers
5. Students
6. Men

Topic list 2
1. Women
2. Babies
3. Dogs
4. Cars
5. Policemen
6. Priests

Topic list 3
1. Cats
2. Doctors
3. Americans
4. Pop groups
5. Actors
6. Politicians

Topic list 4
1. Artists
2. Schools
3. Wild animals
4. TV News Readers
5. Hamburgers
6. Money

Topic list 5
1. Third World countries
2. Vegetarians
3. People who believe in capital punishment
4. People who live in flats
5. Foreigners to my country
6. Fitness fanatics

Generalising

In general,

Generally speaking,

As a rule,

By and large,

In my experience,

Exceptions

There are exceptions of course.

One exception is . . .

But what about . . .

But don't forget . . .

Let's not forget . . .

For example,

For instance,

Take the way (he) . . .

Take for example . . .

For one thing . . .

To give you an idea . . .

Look at the way . . .

**¹By way of
illustration . . .**

45. Illustrating your Point

**Our teacher's a real show-off. Look at the way he drives up
in his Rolls-Royce!**

**The party was a real disaster. To give you an idea of how bad
it was — everyone had left by 10 o'clock!**

In conversation we very often want to illustrate what we are saying
with an example. If we tell a friend that our teacher is 'a bore',
we can't leave it there. The other person wants to know more.
The phrases in the list will help you to introduce the extra information.

On the next page there are lists of words used to describe people.
Use your dictionary to look up words which are new to you. Learn
the ones you think will be useful to you.

Complete the following descriptions:

1. You wouldn't believe what peculiar people I used to work with.
Take my old boss. He was a real _____. For instance,
he used to _____.

2. I suppose it takes all types to make a world. The other week
we were visiting some of my father's family. We haven't seen them
for about 10 years. The oldest son, for example, was a complete
_____. To give you an idea, he _____.

3. You should have been at Peter's party. There was a guy there
who was so _____ you just couldn't believe it. He was
a real _____. Take for example the way he
_____. He _____.

4. Write a description of someone you know.

1. Formal, only for business
meetings etc.

Describing people

Knowledge
intellectual
genius
whiz-kid
egghead
a (computer) buff
bookworm

Humour
comic
a laugh
buffoon
clown
joker
a giggle

Experts
connoisseur
artist
gourmet
guru
expert
educated

Politics
activist
chauvinist
nationalist
revolutionary
liberal
Socialist
Conservative
democrat
conservative with
 a small C

Personality
individualist
worrier
devious
gracious
polite
M. C. P.
feminist
boor
a real gentleman/
 lady

Types
flirt
tease
wolf
casanova
clock-watcher
tramp
down-and-out
hippie
bully
slave driver

Negative words
gossip	nitwit	coward
loudmouth	blockhead	chicken
windbag	thick	wallflower
bore	stupid	sissy
indiscreet	idiot	hypochondriac
snob	hypocrite	drunkard
smart alec	charlatan	glutton
egotist	quack	lecher
primadonna	liar	sex-maniac
creep	do-gooder	grumbler
drip	go-getter	complainer
twit	show-off	pain in the neck

Hesitation Phrases:

Well, um . . .

Well, let's see.

Mmm, I'll have to think about that.

Re-stating:

So what you're saying is . . .

So what you're really saying is . . .

In other words,

If I understand you correctly,

So you mean that . . .

46. What you really mean

Imagine you are a journalist interviewing a politician for a newspaper article.

Journalist: **What are you going to do about the slums?**

Politician: **Well, let me think . . . that is a very difficult question.**

Journalist: **In other words, you don't have any plans.**

When we are asked a question which we either do not know the answer to or which we would prefer to avoid, we often use a hesitation phrase.

If someone insists on finding out our opinion, they can re-state what they think we believe.

Work in pairs as journalist and politician with the following interview questions. Use the phrases in the lists and make conversations like the example above.

Issue 1 — The New Nuclear Power Station

1. What is your opinion of nuclear power?

2. Are you in favour of the new nuclear power station being built 10 miles away?

3. Do you think it will cause health problems for the people in neighbouring villages?

4. What is happening to the people who have to leave their homes to make way for the power station?

5. Why have all the decisions been taken in secret?

Issue 2 — Houses for the Homeless

A large empty building in the centre of town has been occupied by squatters — people with nowhere to live.

1. Do you have plans to bring in the army to evict the squatters?

2. Is it true that you have cut off the water to the building?

3. Do you know that there are women with babies in the building?

4. Where are you going to put these people when they finally come out?

47. Finish your Story

All good stories have to come to an end. The phrases in the list give you ways of drawing your story to an end.

Here are two stories about two people and the first time they smoked. Finish each story.

Story 1

"I remember that my grandfather used to smoke huge Havana cigars. He always bought them in boxes which he kept in the kitchen cupboard. One day when he was in the garden with my grandmother, my brother and I crept into the kitchen and opened the cigar cupboard. We took one of them and hid out in the woods. We took ages trying to light it. After a few puffs we were both violently sick. When we found the courage to go back, our grandmother smelled the cigar on our breath. She was a wise woman and realised what we had been up to. She made us eat some garlic so that grandfather wouldn't find out."

Add a phrase and finish the story.

Story 2

"When I was at school, some of the other boys said you could smoke cinnamon sticks. We were too young to buy cigarettes, but anyone could go into a chemist's shop and buy cinnamon sticks. You said that your mother needed them for cooking. So I decided on my first experiment with smoking. In I went and nervously paid for the cinnamon sticks. I waited till there was no one else at home one day before taking them out and trying to smoke. They tasted horrible! I sat on my bed and tried and tried. So I thought to myself, 'This isn't worth it unless it makes me look older'. So I went into the bathroom and looked at myself in the mirror — bright red with bloodshot eyes. I had to admit that I looked like the silly little boy that I was."

Add a phrase and finish the story.

Story 3

Now tell the class about the first time you yourself did something forbidden. Use one of the phrases from the list to finish the story.

Discussion

Do you feel guilty about the story you have told?
Children are always going to disobey rules.
Why do we bother to give them rules?

To cut a long story short,

So in the end,

So, in short,

So,

To sum up,

All in all,

To put the whole thing in a nutshell,

3. Responding Gambits

If someone asks you a question, you answer it if you can. But conversations do not consist of questions and answers. We very rarely ask direct questions. We make observations and pass comments. We expect other people to respond to us. How they respond tells us how to develop what we say. This means that successful conversations depend partly on how we respond to what other people say. For example, if you disagree very strongly with what someone says, you could say *You must be joking!* and the other person knows that you are surprised — this will make the person think more carefully before continuing.

The gambits in this section allow you to agree or disagree at different levels, to show surprise, disbelief, or polite interest. Among the most useful gambits are *Sorry, I don't follow you.* — to get people to repeat what they said, and *Really?* to get them to develop what they said.

If you learn the responses in this section, other people will find you much easier to talk to and you will find yourself more relaxed and fluent in conversation.

Correct

That's right.

Right.

OK.

Yes.

Exactly!

Wrong

No, I'm afraid not.

Not quite.

You're close.

??????

I don't know.

I'm not sure.

48. Right or wrong

There are many ways of saying that a person is right or wrong about a piece of factual information.

Work in pairs or small groups of 3 or 4 saying what each of the following signs and abbreviations means. Your partners will tell you whether you are right or wrong by using one of the phrases from the list.

Traffic Signs

1.

2.

3.

4.

5.

6.

Mathematical Signs

1. $\pm$

8. $\div$

9. $\rightarrow \infty$

10. $\sqrt{}$

11. $>$

12. $\stackrel{\frown}{=}$

Abbreviations

13. cm
14. °C
15. etc
16. PS
17. MP
18. PM
19. BC
20. Ph.D
21. TV
22. RSVP
23. IOU
24. POW
25. ETA
26. COD
27. DC
28. hp
29. mph
30. UN
31. WHO
32. GNP
33. MD
34. LTD
35. EEC
36. NATO
37. CD
38. Pta
39. %
40. PLC

Answers on page 95.

49. Crowd Reactions

Sometimes we agree or disagree with someone so strongly that we want to say so while he or she is talking.

As a class write down views which are controversial. You can use the ideas below. When these views are ready, anybody in the class who feels strongly about any one of them should stand up and state it strongly and say why. The rest of the class should use the phrases in the list to agree or disagree.

For example:

I don't believe in examinations.
— Come on! Don't be silly!
They're just a waste of time and they're no good for anybody.
— Hear, hear. I agree with you.

Controversial topics.

1. School food.
2. Facilities in the school.
3. Tests and examinations.
4. Adverts on TV.
5. A woman's place is in the home.
6. Murderers should be hanged.
7. Football only creates violence.
8. The tax on cigarettes should be doubled.
9. People who attack children need to be understood — not put into prison.
10. You should be allowed to park wherever you want.
11. All trains and buses should be free to people over the age of 65.
12. No planes should be allowed to fly at night.
13. France is for the French; Germany is for the Germans. Stop all immigration.
14. Men should be paid more than women. They work harder.
15. Passports should be abolished. Who needs them?

Agreeing

Hear! Hear!

You're absolutely right!

[1]You said it!

I agree!

[2]So do I!

[2]Neither can I!

Disagreeing

That's just not true!

Oh, come on!

Rubbish!

Don't give us that!

1. Informal — can only be used with friends.

2. You repeat the auxiliary verb used by the other person, or, if they do not use an auxiliary, you use *do*.

Agreeing

That's (very) true.

I agree with you there.

Yes, I know exactly what you mean.

Disagreeing

Yes, but don't you think . . .

I agree with you, but . . .

Yes, but on the other hand . . .

¹I don't see it quite like that.

50. Getting to Know Someone

One of the main ways we get to know someone better is when we find out what they believe — especially if the person agrees with us.

Work in pairs. Try to think up the advantages and disadvantages of the following ideas. Offer your opinions to your partner and see if you agree or disagree. Take it in turns. Use the phrases in the list.

For example:

The main advantage to being poor is that you don't have to worry about income tax.
— That's very true. But I wonder if it's as simple as that.

Situations

1. Being single/married.
2. Living together.
3. Living in the city/country.
4. Growing a beard.
5. Being poor/rich.
6. Having children.
7. Living near a pub.
8. Living in the centre of a big town.
9. Having a car.
10. Living in a capital city.
11. Travelling abroad a lot.
12. Abortion.
13. Teaching children to drink alcohol.
14. How to teach young people about AIDS.
15. Buying insurance.

1. This can be quite strong, and a warning.

51. Can I help you?

Sometimes we walk into a shop and know exactly what we want. At other times, we can't make up our minds. We look at something; we check the price; we try it on; and still we can't decide. The list of phrases gives all the language you need if you can't decide.

Work in pairs — one person is the shop assistant, the other is the customer. Work with the following list of purchases and the dialogue skeleton below:

1. a wedding ring
2. a bottle of perfume
3. a car (large or small, two or four doors)
4. a stereo (can you afford CD?)
5. a holiday abroad
6. a dress
7. a tie
8. wallpaper for the living room (colour? pattern?)
9. a record for a friend
10. a shirt (plain/striped/white/coloured/cotton/polyester)

Assistant: Excuse me, can I help you?

Customer: I'm looking for a _____.

Assistant: Size? Colour? Price?

Customer: (You can't decide).

Assistant: Well, what about _____.

Customer: (You still can't decide.)

[1]**I'm afraid I don't know.**

I'm afraid I can't decide.

I'm afraid I can't make up my mind.

I'll have to think about it.

I'm really not sure.

[2]**I think I'll leave it, thank you.**

1. Remember *I'm afraid* is usually added to any response which the listener may find unhelpful.

2. This fixed phrase is used when you want to say you are not going to buy anything and are going to leave the shop.

Strong agreement

Of course I would!

I certainly would!

Mild agreement

I think I would.

I might.

I might consider it.

I think so.

Indecision

I don't know.

I can't decide.

I can't make up my mind.

I'm not sure.

52. The Love Test

Are you a hopeless romantic — willing to do anything for your love? Or are you a down-to-earth realist who accepts life with or without love?

Work in pairs and interview each other using the Love Test on the next page.

Take it in turns to interview each other. One student asks the questions; the other chooses answers from the phrases in the lists. There is a special scoring system below.

Scoring

For questions 2, 4, 6, 8, 10, score as follows:

Strong agreement	1
Mild agreement	2
Indecision	3
Mild disagreement	4
Strong disagreement	5

For questions 1, 3, 5, 7, 9, score as follows:

Strong agreement	5
Mild agreement	4
Indecision	3
Mild disagreement	2
Strong disagreement	1

The Love Test

1. You have a steady partner. Along comes a really attractive person. Could you fall in love with someone else?   Score _____

2. Would you consider marrying someone from a very different background to your own?   Score _____

3. Would you consider writing off to a computer dating firm?   Score _____

4. Do you believe that marriage is for life?   Score _____

5. Would you consider getting married and not having children?   Score _____

6. Would you say no to someone you liked very much — because you thought someone better might come along?   Score _____

7. If the person you love died, would you still consider life worth living?   Score _____

8. Could you fall in love with someone whom you do not find physically attractive?   Score _____

9. Do you agree that "Men are interested in women for one reason and one reason only"?   Score _____

10. Imagine that you have very little money. Would you consider marrying someone who also had very little money?   Score _____

To find out how romantic you are, turn to page 95 for the results.

Total score: _____

Mild disagreement

Probably not.

I don't think so.

I doubt it.

Strong disagreement

Never in a million years!

Not on your life!

Not (even) if you paid me!

Not for all the tea in China!

I'm afraid I don't know.

I'm sorry I don't know.

I haven't a clue.

I couldn't tell you.

I'm not sure.

Oh, it's slipped my mind.

I've forgotten.

It's no good, I can't remember.

53. I haven't a Clue!

Divide the class into two teams. One student asks the questions; another keeps the score. Each team scores 1 point for a correct answer, and two points if a team member uses one of the phrases from the list — admitting that they don't know the answer.

Here are 20 questions. The teams may also spend 15 minutes preparing questions for each other.

Quiz

1. What was the name of the first man on the moon?
2. What exactly were his first words?
3. What year did Man land on the moon?
4. What's the longest river in the world?
5. What country is it in?
6. What is the capital city of Switzerland?
7. Where were the 1980 summer Olympic Games held?
8. How many are there in a dozen?
9. How many are there in a baker's dozen?
10. How many Beatles were there?
11. Where was Elvis Presley born?
12. How many volumes are there in the Encyclopedia Britannica?
13. How far away is the sun?
14. At what speed does Concorde fly?
15. Who invented basketball?
16. What is the weight of a golfball?
17. When did Queen Victoria die?
18. How many bees are there in a normal beehive?
19. What do we call a large group of sheep?
20. What is the population of France to the nearest million?

54. It serves you right

Usually when we hear bad news, we are sympathetic. Sometimes, however, it is difficult to be sympathetic if we feel that the person 'deserved' what happened — for example, if they never lock their car and it is stolen.

Example dialogue:

I've just had my car stolen!
— It serves you right. You should have locked it.

I've just been thrown out of my flat!
— What did you expect? You shouldn't have had so many wild parties.

Work in pairs, taking turns to react. Use these ideas and the phrases in the list.

1. lost your job
   — late most days

2. lost your driving licence
   — always speeding

3. got an electric shock
   — didn't switch off the electricity before trying to mend the light

4. went to sleep during the exam
   — went to a party till 4 in the morning

5. had a fight with Pete
   — rude to him

6. didn't get the £50 back from Bill
   — warned you

7. got lost in Paris
   — told you to take a map

Make up your own responses to the following

8. I've just got a parking ticket.

9. I was ill last night.

10. I was late for the train

11. There's something wrong with my alarm clock.

12. I've just been ignored by Mary.

Discussion

Can you name a misfortune which you 'deserved'.

It serves you right.

It's your own fault.

What did you expect?

Perhaps that'll teach you.

55. Analyse your Handwriting

Many people believe that you can learn a lot about a person if you analyse their handwriting. Whether you believe it or not, if can be great fun.

Work in pairs. One person must agree to be the 'expert' and work with the information on page 74/5.
The other:

1. Take a piece of paper with NO LINES.
2. Write, in your ordinary handwriting, the following two sentences:
   I'm sure that he'll go swimming today.
   Tomorrow it'll be too cold for swimming,
   and then he'll have to go fishing.

Now do the following tests. Only the 'expert' should look at the answers.

Test 1

Hold a ruler below the written lines. Are all the words on the line, like this?

a.

All the words are on the line.

or do they go up and down, like this?

b.

The words go up and down.

The expert decides whether the handwriting matches 1a or 1b, writes it down, reads the interpretation from page 74/5, and records it. Each subject accepts or rejects the analysis making use of a gambit. Now, go on to Test 2.

Test 2

Draw a line below a few words in the middle of the sample. Does it go up or down on·the page? Estimate which of the lines below corresponds best to your partner's slant of writing.

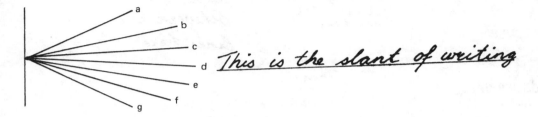

The expert interprets and records the results. The subject responds with a gambit. Continue in this way for each test.

Test 3

Does the handwriting slope to the right, to the left, or is it in-between?

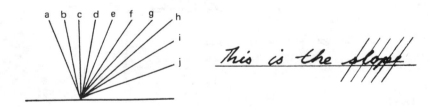

Test 4

Which is the set of parallel lines that fits the small letters?

a. **d.**

b. **e.**

c. **f.**

Agreeing

I'm not surprised.

That doesn't surprise me.

Yes, that sounds like me.

I knew it!

I thought so.

Just what I've always thought.

Absolutely!

Disagreeing

You're joking!

You must be joking!

I don't believe it!

No, definitely not!

Come on!

I don't think so.

I don't think that's very fair

Are you pulling my leg?

That's news to me!

Test 5

Is there little, some or much space between the lines?

a. *There's little space between the lines here.*

b. *There's some space between the lines here.*

c. *There's much space between the lines here.*

Test 6

Check if the letters are usually connected, sometimes disconnected, or usually disconnected.

a. *connected*

b. *sometimes disconnected*

c. *disconnected*

Test 7

Look at the m's in 'swimming':

a. pointed

b. garlands

c. arcades

d. thready

Test 8

Check how even-sized the letters are:

a. varying size

b. same size throughout

c. tapering size

Test 9

Look at the letter 'e' when it comes at the end of a word. What does it generally look like?

a. long final *have*   **b.** short final *have*   **c.** no final *have*   **d.** rising final *have*

e. curling final *have*   **f.** ascending final *have*   **g.** descending final *have*   **h.** dropping final *have*

i. final hooking up *have*   **j.** final hooking down *have*   **k.** short, curving final *have*   **l.** lasso final *have*

Test 10

Check if the letters 'o' and 'a' are usually open or closed.

a. *They're usually open at the top.*

b. *They're sometimes closed at the top.*

c. *They're usually closed at the top.*

Test 11

Find out how the i's are dotted most of the time.

a. dot right over *i*   **f.** wavy dot *i*

b. dot high *i*   **g.** dot flying to the left *i*

c. dot flying to the right *i*   **h.** hook dot *i*

d. circle dot *i*   **i.** dash dot *i*

e. thick dot *i*   **j.** no dot *i*

Test 12

Compare how the t's are crossed in most cases.

a. bar to the right *t*   **f.** looped bar *t*

b. bar to the left *t*   **g.** down-slant bar *t*

c. bar centered *t*   **h.** up-slant bar, high *t*

d. bar high left *t*   **i.** heavy bar *t*

e. star cross *t*   **j.** bar missing *t*

Agreeing

I'm not surprised.

That doesn't surprise me.

Yes, that sounds like me.

I knew it!

I thought so.

Just what I've always thought.

Absolutely!

Disagreeing

You're joking!

You must be joking!

I don't believe it!

No, definitely not!

Come on!

I don't think so.

I don't think that's very fair

Are you pulling my leg?

That's news to me!

Interpretation of handwriting analysis

1a	straightforward, dependable, systematic
1b	unsystematic, carefree, versatile
2a	exuberant, optimistic (sometimes temporarily)
2b	ambitious, optimistic
2c	firm, confident
2d	no special characteristics indicated
2e	passive, unhappy (sometimes temporarily)
2f	gloomy, pessimistic
2g	very unhappy, despondent
3a or b	self conscious, ego-centric, analytic
3c	emotionless, reserved
3d or e	no special characteristics indicated
3f, g, or h	generous, spontaneous, friendly
3i or j	eager, impulsive
4a or b	intellectual, rational, unassertive
4c	no special characteristics indicated
4d, e, or f	generous, restless, somewhat inattentive, assertive
5a	confused, unclear
5b	clear, organized
5c	good at organization, generous
6a	logical, adaptable
6b	mixed rational-intuitive
6c	meticulous, unadaptable, somewhat impractical
7a	energetic, competitive
	together with 1b, and 2c, and 4a or b*: eccentric
	together with 2b: enthusiastic
	together with 3c, and 4a or b, and 5c and 6a: discerning, careful
	together with 3f, g, or h: lively
	together with 5c, and 6b: wise
7b	adaptable, receptive to new ideas, pleasure-loving
	together with 2b*: enthusiastic
7c	reserved, strong-willed
	together with 1b, and 2e, and 3c*: careless
7d	intelligent, creative
	together with 1b, and 4a or b*: creative
	together with 1b, and 2c, and 4a or b: eccentric
8a	changeable
	together with 1b, and 4a or b: versatile
8b	conscientious
	together with 1a: honest
8c	tactful, discreet
9a	self-confident
9b	reserved
9c	self-centered
9d	interested in musical matters
9e	protective, sensitive
9f	friendly
9g	timid, shy
9h	passive
9i or j	tenacious, stubborn
	together with 1b, and 7a, and 8a: sly
	together with 3c: interested in possessions

	together with 4a or b: petty
9k	fun-loving
9l	critical

10a	frank, outspoken
10b	sincere
	together with 1a, and 8b, frank, outspoken
10c	secretive
	together with 4a or b, and 5c, and 7a: critical

11a	meticulous, precise together with 8b: very conscientious
11b	imaginative, enthusiastic
11c	impulsive, intuitive
11d	having artistic interests, sometimes demanding attention
11e	aggressive , materialistic
11f	humorous
11g	hesitant, cautious
11h	witty, perceptive
11i	impatient
	together with 4a or b: fussy
11j	absent-minded, careless

12a	impulsive, quick, lively
12b	procrastinating
	together with 8a: indecisive
12c	controlled, careful
	together with 2c, and 7a or b, and 9f or i: very determined
	together with 1a, and 9a or f: independent
12d	insecure
12e	very sensitive
12f	persistent
12g	opinionated, critical
12h	ambitious
12i	strong-willed
	together with 2c, and 7a or b, and 9f or i: very determined
	together with 3c: arrogant
	together with 7a: aggressive
12j	careless, absent-minded

Caution: Even the best handwriting analysis cannot fully describe a person's character. One study, for instance, showed a maximum accuracy of only 75%. It is therefore best not to take this game too seriously.

*In combinations, all noted elements must be present.

When you are surprised

[1]Really!

Are you joking?

Oh?

Where? Show me.

I can't see that.

Goodness!

What?

When you agree

So [2]do I.

Me too!

That's what I thought too!

But that's what I was going to say.

56. Inkblots

What do you see in these inkblots? Some people see people, animals, faces or trees. Some people can't see anything at all.

Work in pairs and tell each other what you can see. If you can't see anything at all, try to relax, and let your imagination work. React to each other's ideas using a phrase from the list.

Finally, share your ideas together with the whole class.

For example:

Maria said she saw two horses laughing at each other in the seventh inkblot.
—That's what I thought too!

or

I see a cat looking through some bushes.
—Really!

1.

2.

1. This expression is often used to make the other person say more. This single word is usually enough to do that.

2. Or, you repeat the other person's auxiliary verb: *So can I.*

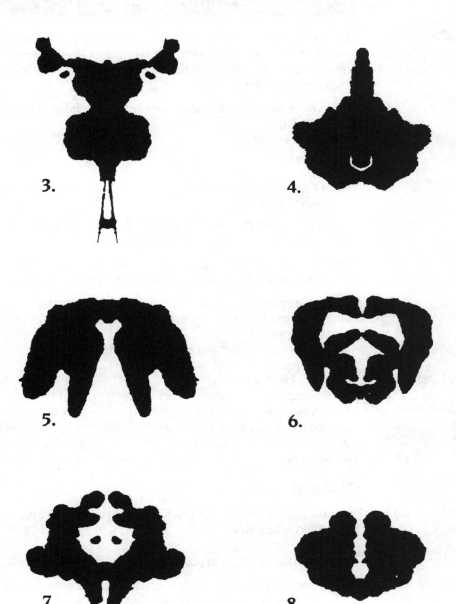

3.

4.

5.

6.

7.

8.

Less serious news

Oh no!

What a pity!

What a shame.

What a nuisance.

Poor you.

Very sad news

How awful!

How terrible!

I'm really sorry to hear that.

That must've been awful!

57. Being Sympathetic

How do we react when we have some bad news? It depends on the news. Some things are more important than others, and we react to something serious in a different way from something less serious, however unfortunate.

Have you heard that 300 people were killed when a plane crashed this morning?
—Oh, how terrible!

and

I didn't get the job after all.
—Oh, what a pity!

If you reacted to the first situation with *What a pity*, people would think that you were a strange person indeed!

Work in pairs with these sentences. One person give the news; the other react in an appropriate way using a phrase from the list.

1. My girlfriend . . . . sprained . . . . ankle . . . . first day . . . . holiday.
2. Someone I knew . . . . had . . . . all his money . . . . stolen . . . . jacket pocket.
3. My uncle . . . . passed away . . . . last week.
4. Someone I know at work . . . . told . . . . cancer.
5. I . . . . bike stolen.
6. Someone . . . . stole . . . . car radio . . . . lunchtime.
7. Several hundred people . . . . killed . . . . yesterday's earthquake.
8. Someone pinched . . . . passport . . . . all my cash . . . . hotel room.
9. A colleague . . . : made redundant . . . . 25 years . . . . same company.
10. My sister . . . . hit . . . . mouth . . . . car door . . . . broke a tooth.

Discussion

Talk about what you say AND what you do when you hear very bad news in your country.

1. What would you say in your language in the following situations:

   a. A friend tells you that there has just been a terrible earthquake — thousands of people are dead.
   b. A friend tells you that she has just heard that her mother has died.
   c. A friend tells you that his house has been burgled.
   d. A friend tells you that he has to go to the dentist this afternoon.
   e. A friend tells you that his wife's car broke down in the very centre of town.

2. In your country do people DO something different when they hear a piece of bad news?

58. The Interview

In groups of 3 or 4 prepare to hold an interview for a job. Decide who will be the applicant and who will be the 'interviewing board'.

The applicant: you have been manager of a medium-sized supermarket in the centre of town for 10 years. You think you have been successful and a good boss. When the interviewers ask a question, use one of the phrases from the list. The phrases will give you a little more time to think of your answer.

The interviewers: you own a large department store in the centre of town. It employs 200 people. The manager has just resigned. You are interviewing the applicant for the post of manager. Use the questions below or think up your own questions. Take turns to ask the questions.

Questions

1. Why would you like to leave your present job?
2. Say a little about the work you do.
3. How long have you been manager?
4. What is the worst problem you have had in your present job?
5. What makes you think you will enjoy this new job?
6. Do you think you are popular with the people who work for you?
7. If you could choose your own boss, what kind of person would you choose?
8. If you didn't agree with your boss about something important, what would you do?
9. Think of the situation where one of your employees was late for work three days out of four. He is a very good worker. What would you do?
10. What do you think you will be doing in 10 years time?
11. What do you do in your spare time?
12. How much do you think we should pay you?

Well, let me see.

Well, let me think.

I'll have to think about that.

That's a good question.

How shall I put it?

Let's put it this way.

The best way I can answer that is . . .

Mm, that's a difficult question. Let me see.

Right.

OK.

Yes?

And?

¹Really?

And then?

Auxiliaries:

²Did you?

Have you?

Are you?

Were you?

Was it?

. . . .

59. Showing Interest

When we listen to other people, we often want to show them how interested we are in their conversation. We do this in different ways:

    smiling with our eyes
    nodding
    saying something encouraging

Work in pairs. One student describes an exciting or amusing event from the list of ideas below — or something real; the other student responds in the three ways. Use phrases from the list. Use the phrases *while* the other person is speaking. Don't wait for pauses or for the other person to finish speaking.

Ideas

1. The day I won a million.
2. My favourite holiday.
3. My worst day ever.
4. The best meal I've ever had.
5. How we share the work in my home.
6. My first trip to Britain/America.
7. My worst day at school.
8. Something really good that has happened to you.
9. Something really embarrassing.
10. Your story.

1. This single word is the easiest way to make another person continue with their story, or to expand on what they have already said.

2. You repeat the auxiliary that the previous speaker has used. The effect is the same as using *Really?*.

60. Are you following me?

If we have to listen to something long and complicated, we may want to ask the speaker to repeat what was said.

And if we are the person giving the information, we may want to check that the other person has understood correctly.

Work in small groups of 3 or 4. Take it in turns for one person to read the problems below. That person should use the 'checking gambits'. The listeners should use the 'repetition gambits'.

Problems

1. Start with 5, multiply by 4, divide that by 2, subtract 3, then multiply by 10, then take half of that. What do you get?

2. If you write with your left hand, but draw with the opposite hand, and kick a ball with the foot on the same side, yet put the phone to your ear on the other side, which is the side where you are short-sighted, which eye is your good eye?

3. So you want go to the stadium. Well, it's quite a long way, actually. Go straight along here till you get to the traffic lights, not the first set, the second set, then turn right, then the second on the left, then it's a straight road for about a mile till you get to the Odeon Cinema. Just past the Odeon, there's a big roundabout, go straight across it, and the stadium is in the park a couple of hundred yards on the left. It's not difficult to find!

4. Assume you have a tower made up of four building blocks: at the bottom there is a cube, then there is an octahedron (eight-faced solid), on top of which there is a cylinder, and at the very top there is a pyramid. Now suppose you put the cylinder underneath the octahedron. Then you put the cube below the pyramid. Then you put the octahedron at the bottom of the whole pile. What is the sequence of building blocks now?

5. Make up your own problem and present it to your group. Make notes to help you.

Repetition Gambits

Would you mind repeating that?

Sorry, I didn't catch the last part.

Sorry, you've lost me.

Sorry, I don't follow you.

What was that again?

Checking Gambits

Are you with me?

Are you still with me?

Is that clear?

OK so far?

Have you got it?

Do you understand so far?

82

Sorry, what did you say?

¹Sorry?

I didn't get the bit about . . .

I'm sorry I can't hear you. It's a very bad line.

1. Remember speakers of British English do not use *Excuse me* in this meaning. For them, *Excuse me* is used before they disturb somebody, and only *Sorry?* or *Pardon?* are possible here.

61. Communication Problems

It is very easy to misunderstand someone on the telephone. We can't see the person we are speaking to. The line can be bad. There may be other noises around us. In this difficult situation, we use the phrases in the list.

Work in pairs with these serious situations. Correct communication is essential. One student is the telephone receptionist for emergencies. Take it in turns to be the caller.

Situation 1 — Fire

Caller: This is an emergency. There is a fire on the sixth floor of my block. I live on the fifth floor and there are clouds of smoke coming out of the flat above me (flat 609, 25 Sussex Drive). The hall outside my flat is filling with smoke.
Switchboard: Get the name, address, flat number, type of building. Find out if flames are visible. Tell the caller to set off the fire alarm and make sure to use the stairs, not the lift. Say the fire brigade is on its way.

Situation 2 — Police

Caller: There's a fight in a bar at 313 King Street between a big fat guy with enormous muscles and a small fat guy with a moustache who looks like a professional wrestler. They're using knives. One of them has a gun. The big guy is bleeding badly.
Police station: Get the address of the bar, a description of the men, and the name and address of the caller. Tell him that a police car will be there within minutes.

Situation 3 — The Vet

Caller: You went into your bathroom and found a huge boa constrictor in the bath. The snake didn't move, and you played it cool. You closed the window and the bathroom door. You live at 104 Farnham Crescent.
Vet: Get the name and address of the caller. Tell him to put the toilet seat down, keep the bathroom door shut. A snake specialist will be there in two hours time.

Situation 4 — the Hospital

Caller: Your wife is having a heart attack. She is feeling severe pain in her chest and left arm. She is sweating heavily, and is very short of breath. You live in flat 3a, 48 Regency Road.
Hospital: Get the address and tell the caller that an ambulance will be on its way straightaway. Tell him to give his wife artificial respiration, to keep her in a sitting-position, but not to move her too much.

Situation 5

Think of an emergency situation which you have been involved in yourself. Act out the situation with a telephone receptionist.

Discussion

Have you ever been involved in a real-life emergency?
Tell the others about it.
Did you do the right thing?

Would you mind saying that again?

Could you repeat your address, please?

Could you spell it, please?

Oh, thank you.

That's very kind of you.

It's very kind of you to say that.

Do you really think so?

Thanks. I needed that.

You've made my day!

62. Accepting a Compliment

Are you good at accepting a compliment — or do you become embarrassed? Accepting a compliment is sometimes more difficult than paying one!

Work in pairs, paying and accepting compliments in turn. You may use your own ideas or the ideas below.

For example:

> **I really like your dress Marie.**
> **Oh, thank you. I bought it at that new shop that's just opened.**

Marie was pleased and added extra information — the dress was new. But sometimes we want to 'play down' the compliment.

For example:

> **I really like your dress Marie.**
> **Oh, thank you. I've had it for years.**

Ideas for compliments

1. a dress
2. a shirt
3. a new car
4. a fancy tie
5. very neat handwriting
6. the way someone's had their hair done
7. a new house/flat
8. a meal
9. English pronunciation
10. a ring

Match these 10 ideas with the following ways of 'playing down' a compliment:

a. Oh, it took no time at all.
b. My boyfriend gave it to me.
c. I've just changed my hairdresser.
d. It's from Marks & Spencers.
e. I'm not too keen on the colour myself.
f. I spent a year in the States.
g. I hope it's not too vulgar!
h. It took us a long time to find it.
i. I was taught very well.
j. But it uses too much petrol.

63. Mini-Conversations

Most of the activites in this book help you to practise the gambits for one or two "bits" of a conversation. But you might like to build longer "mini-conversations" to remind you of some of the gambits you have practised earlier.

On these few pages you will find suggestions for some mini-conversations which you can practise in pairs.

Remember, the idea is to practise the gambits. If you are short of ideas for the content of your conversations, use one or more of the subjects on pages 89 to 93.

1.

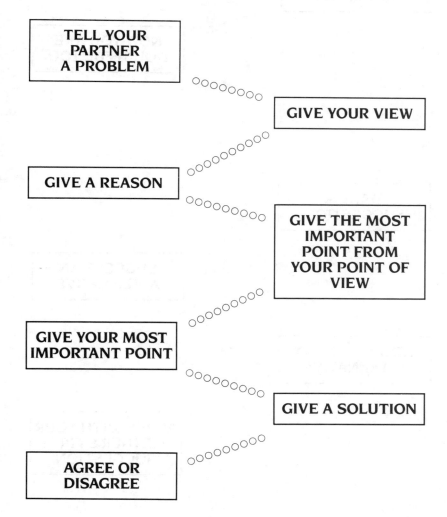

2.

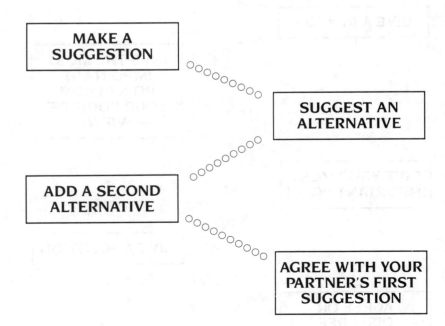

SAY SOMETHING YOU ARE CERTAIN OF

YOU ARE DOUBTFUL

GIVE A STRONG ARGUMENT

NOW YOU ARE DOUBTFUL TOO

3.

MAKE A SUGGESTION

SUGGEST AN ALTERNATIVE

ADD A SECOND ALTERNATIVE

AGREE WITH YOUR PARTNER'S FIRST SUGGESTION

4.

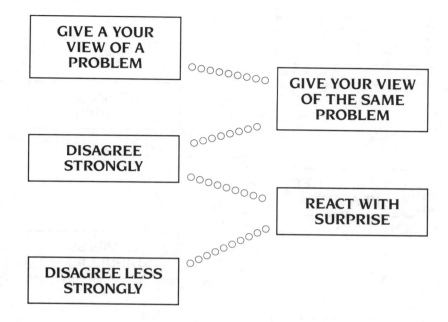

5.

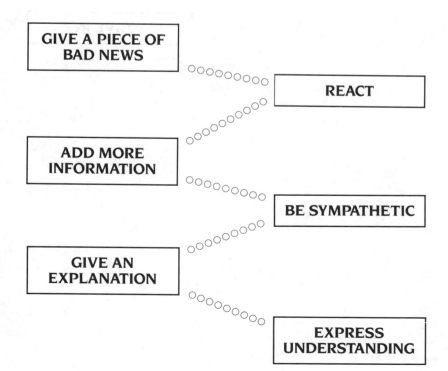

6.

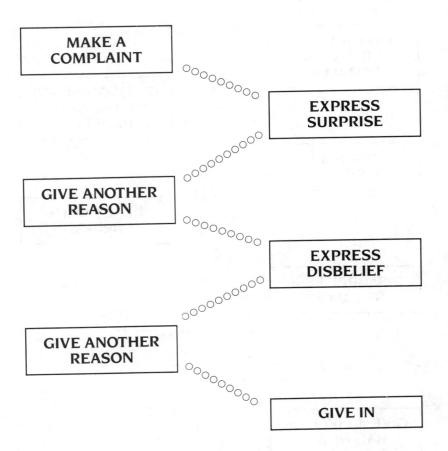

MAKE A COMPLAINT

EXPRESS SURPRISE

GIVE ANOTHER REASON

EXPRESS DISBELIEF

GIVE ANOTHER REASON

GIVE IN

Subjects

Remember, in all the activities in this book, it is more important to practise the *Conversation Gambits* — The language is more important, while you are practising, than the content of what you say!

Sometimes you may have trouble thinking of ideas for the content of some of the practices. To help you, here are 30 subjects with a few important ideas connected with each. You can use any of these subjects for the mini-conversations (pages 85 to 88), or for many of the other activities in the book.

Television

Too much violence
Trivial programmes
Kills conversation
Makes people passive

Good value for money
Terrific source of news
Very educational
Helps lonely people

Living in the country

Isolated and lonely
Dull and boring
OK in summer, awful in winter
Too many insects

Neighbours help each other more
Surrounded by nature
No stress or pressure
Fresh air

Healthy eating

I know what's best for me
Enjoyment more important
Boring and tasteless
Only for fanatics

Think of the future
Good for you
Avoid cancer

Teenage drug abuse

Parents to blame
Heavy fines
Prison
Sign of the times

Got to understand why
Care in special centres
Long-term problem

Aid to the Third World

Guns, armies, weapons
Irresponsible leaders
Charity begins at home
Corruption

Responsibility
Famine, starvation
Malnutrition
Caring and sharing

Cars

Pollution
Carbon monoxide
Accidents
Status symbol

A necessity
Freedom
Mobile
The modern world

Politics

Only for the power-crazy
Power corrupts
Career politicians
A necessary evil

Involvement
Party politics
Democracy
Alternative?

Nuclear power

Dangerous
Waste from nuclear reactor
Contamination
Threat to the world

The nuclear age
Cheap source of energy
Remote places
Best available

Living in the city

Noisy, dirty, unhealthy
Traffic, danger
Pace of life, stress
Too many people

Always something happening
Stimulating, exciting
Night life
Plenty of variety

Old buildings

Should be demolished
The price of progress
Old-fashioned, cold
Waste energy

Add character
Conservation
Human design
Concrete jungle

To strike or not to strike

Very low wages
Can only take holidays in winter
Atmosphere is too dusty, unhealthy
Firm made huge profits last year

Boss is very nice
Good food in the canteen
Easy to take time off to go to dentist
Bonus at Christmas

Reporting an accident

Volvo driver was to blame
Volvo was going too slowly
The old lady didn't look before crossing
Traffic lights weren't working

Lorry overtook on the crossing
Speed limit
It was getting dark
Difficult to say

Describing the man who ran away

Tall
Darkish hair
Not from this part of the country
Dark suit

Above average height
Black straight hair
Welsh accent
Quite well-dressed

The ideal teacher

Strict
Lots of homework
Properly dressed
Talks a lot, but students must be silent

Progressive
Up-to-date, modern approach
Jeans, no tie
Allows students to talk

Prisons

Too comfortable
Deterrent
Made to suffer
The taxpayers' money

Basic human rights
Dignity
Home comforts
Understanding

Smoking

Stink
Lung cancer
Selfish
The expense

Freedom of the individual
My right to decide
Nervous

God

Man created God
No need
No life after death
Superstition

God created Man
Belief
Meaning to life
Church

Sex education in schools

In the home
Not what schools are for
How far do you go?
Love more important than sex

Who else could teach it?
Unwanted pregnancy
Responsible attitudes
Mature

The green movement

Bunch of crackpots
Out of date
Unrealistic
Uneconomic

Peace-loving
Destruction of the environment
Forest, whales, clean air
Global village

Dogs

Fouling the streets
Penalty
Unhealthy for children
Bite, rabies, deaths

Man's best friend
Companionship, guide dogs
The old and the lonely
Faithful, sheep dogs

Volcano

Mt Etna has erupted
Hundreds dead
Thousands homeless

Last time was 1958
Terrible
Horrific

Air crash

Two jumbo jets
650 people
Mid-air collision
Thunder storm

Awful
Unthinkable

Funeral

Off work tomorrow
Uncle's funeral
95
Long illness

What is wrong?
Old?

Trouble at home

Teenage son in trouble with police
Stole a car
16
Crazy about cars

Stealing?
Age?
Sorry?

Complaints

1. Typewriter, £200
   3 letters don't work
   Very careful
   Only 1 week old

   Very reliable
   Have you dropped it?
   Very good make

2. Car, £8,000
   Terrible noise
   Worst in 4th gear

   Beautiful model
   Don't understand
   Investigate

3. Dress, £45
   Hole under arm
   Refund?
   Only prepared to accept a refund or replacement
   but not a repair

   Receipt?
   Don't understand, carefully checked
   No refund, but will repair

4. Holiday in Turkey, £550
   Hotel was awful
   Had to share a room!
   Return flight was 23 hours late
   Refund?
   Want £50 NOW

   Should have phoned from Turkey
   Should have complained to
   representative
   £50 off next year's holiday

Teenage problems

Parents should be stricter
Home by 10.30pm latest
Stop pocket-money if problems
Remind what things were like when you were young

Trust your children
Home by midnight
Talk problems through as a family
Be a friend, not a parent

Persuading

Come to the party
Fun
Dancing
Good food
Great music
Sue will be there

Rather not
Shy
Can't
Can eat at home
Got better at home
Think about it

Buying a new stereo

Best value for money
Good amplifier
40 watt speakers
Special offer at moment
£100 off

Bit expensive
Doesn't look attractive
Too big for my room
Sounds better
OK

Planning a trip to the tropics

Innoculations, visas, sun cream, pills, light clothes, mosquito net, insect repellent, cotton underwear, phrase book, guide books

Answers

The Love Test — Scores

10-20: You're a hopeless romantic.
21-39: You have both romantic and realistic tendencies.
40-50: You are a dry realist.

48. Right or Wrong — Answers

1. no entry 2. no left turn. 3. no U turns. 4. speed limit 40
5. bicycles only 6. parking restricted to owners of special permits
7. plus or minus 8. divide 9. tends to infinity 10. square root
11. is greater than 12. is approximately equal to 13. centi-
metre 14. degrees centigrade 15. etcetera 16. postscript
(something added at the end of a letter) 17. Member of
Parliament/Military Police 18. Prime Minister 19. before
Christ 20. Doctor of Philosophy 21. television 22. please reply
23. I owe you 24. prisoner of war 25. estimated time of
arrival 26. cash on delivery 27. direct current 28. horse power
29. miles per hour 30. United Nations 31. World Health
Organisation 32. gross national product 33. Managing
Director 34. limited 35. European Economic Community
36. North Atlantic Treaty Organisation 37. compact disc
38. peseta 39. percent 40. public limited company.

Language Teaching Publications
35 Church Road, Hove, BN3 2BE

© **Language Teaching Publications 1988**
ISBN 0 906717 59 0

Drawings by Aili Kuris

Edited by Jimmie Hill

Originally published by the Public Service Commission of Canada under the titles Gambits 1, 2, 3 as part of Contact Canada, © Minister of Supply and Services Canada. The original Canadian editions can be ordered from:
The Canadian Government Publishing Centre
Supply and Services Canada
Ottawa
Canada KA1 0S9

Printed in England by Commercial Colour Press Plc, London E7.
Reprinted 1998

Conversation Gambits

Eric Keller and Sylvia T Warner

Real English Conversation Practices

Language Teaching Publications

Contents